WILLIAMS-SONOMA

FOODMADEFAST
seafood

RECIPES
Jay Harlow

GENERAL EDITOR
Chuck Williams

PHOTOGRAPHY
Bill Bettencourt

Oxmoor House®

contents

fish

shellfish

about this book

It will come as no surprise that seafood is a natural favorite of the busy cook. It is not only easy to prepare, but is also healthy and delicious. Each carefully crafted recipe in Food Made Fast *Seafood* calls for just a handful of easy-to-find ingredients and requires remarkably little work to put a satisfying dish on the dinner table.

In this book, you will find classic and contemporary recipes for both fish and shellfish, most of which take less than 30 minutes to prepare from start to finish. Others require only 15 minutes of hands-on time. There is buttery Trout Amandine or creamy Linguine with Shrimp for nights when company is coming, and Fish Tacos or Tilapia with Sweet Peppers for hectic weeknights when time is especially short. You can round out each menu with a salad, a simple vegetable side dish, or bread, and you'll have a home-cooked meal that has taken only minutes to prepare.

Chuck

FISH 30 minutes
start to finish

trout
amandine

Trout fillets, 4, 1½ lb
(750 g) total weight

**Salt and freshly ground
pepper**

Slivered almonds, ¼ cup
(1 oz/30 g)

Flour, ⅓ cup (2 oz/60 g)

Olive oil, 2 tablespoons

Unsalted butter,
4 tablespoons (2 oz/60 g)

Lemon juice, from 1 lemon

**Fresh flat-leaf (Italian)
parsley,** ¼ cup (⅓ oz/10 g)
minced

SERVES 4

1 Season the trout and toast the almonds
Place the fillets on a plate and season on both sides
with salt and pepper; set aside. Heat a large frying pan
over medium-low heat. Add the almonds and toast, stirring
frequently, until they turn light tan, 3–5 minutes. Transfer
to a plate.

2 Cook the trout
Return the pan to medium-low heat. Spread the flour
on a large plate and dip the fillets in the flour, coating both
sides well and shaking off any excess. Add the oil to the pan
and raise the heat to medium. Add the fillets, skin side up,
and cook until browned, about 4 minutes. Turn and cook until
the fillets flake easily near the tail ends, about 2 minutes
longer. Transfer the fillets, skin side down, to individual plates
and keep warm.

3 Make the sauce
Wipe any oil from the pan with a paper towel. Return
the pan to medium heat and add the butter. When the butter
has melted, add the lemon juice and parsley. Stir in the
almonds and season to taste with salt and pepper. Spoon
the sauce over the fillets and serve.

cook's tip

It is important that the trout in
this recipe—and any fish prepared
in a frying pan on the stove top—
cook evenly. To ensure even
cooking, when you turn the fillets,
exchange those in the center,
where the heat is most intense,
with those near the sides of
the pan. This recipe also works
well with sole, flounder, or tilapia.

cook's tip

Supermarkets, farmers' markets, and ethnic markets carry an ever larger array of prepared salsas, from mild to hot, based on tomatoes

or tomatillos, and including countless chile varieties. Salsas sold refrigerated in plastic tubs often have a fresher taste and texture than those in cans or jars. Sample what is available where you live until you find one you like.

fish tacos

1 Season the fish
If using tilapia, split the fillets lengthwise along the seam. Place the fish on a plate. In a small bowl, combine the cumin, oregano, and ½ teaspoon salt. Sprinkle over both sides of the fish. Drizzle with the oil and lime juice.

2 Heat the tortillas
Preheat a cast-iron or other heavy frying pan over medium-low heat, and a stovetop grill pan over medium-low heat on another burner. One at a time, warm the tortillas in the frying pan until flexible. Stack them on a plate and cover with a clean kitchen towel.

3 Cook the fish and assemble the tacos
Raise the heat under the grill pan to medium-high. When the pan is hot, add the fish and cook until golden, about 3 minutes. Turn and cook until golden around the edges, 1–2 minutes longer, depending on type and thickness. Transfer the fish to a plate and cut into bite-sized pieces. Place an equal amount of the fish on each warm tortilla and top with shredded cabbage, a spoonful of salsa, and a drizzle of sour cream. Sprinkle with cilantro and serve.

Tilapia, cod, or other mild white-fleshed fish fillets, 1 lb (500 g)

Ground cumin, ¼ teaspoon

Dried oregano, ¼ teaspoon

Salt

Olive oil, 1 tablespoon

Lime juice, from 1 lime

Corn tortillas, 12

Green cabbage, 2 cups (6 oz/185 g) finely shredded

Fresh salsa, 1 cup (8 fl oz/ 250 ml), homemade or purchased

Sour cream, ⅓ cup (3 oz/ 90 g), stirred

Fresh cilantro (fresh coriander), 2 tablespoons coarsely chopped

SERVES 4

rockfish in black bean sauce

Canola oil, 1 tablespoon

Ginger, 1 tablespoon minced

Green (spring) onions, 2, white parts minced and green tops thinly sliced

Black bean sauce, 1 tablespoon

Chicken broth, ½ cup (4 fl oz/125 ml)

Sugar

Rockfish or other lean white-fleshed fish fillets, 1½ lb (750 g), pin bones removed and fillets thinly sliced

Cornstarch (cornflour), 1 teaspoon

SERVES 4

1 **Prepare the sauce**
In a deep frying pan or wok over medium-low heat, warm the oil. Add the ginger and minced green onions and cook until fragrant, about 15 seconds. Add the black bean sauce, the broth, and a pinch of sugar and bring to a simmer.

2 **Cook the fish**
Add the fish slices to the sauce and simmer until the thinnest slices begin to flake apart, 3–4 minutes. Using a spatula, transfer the fish to plates, leaving most of the sauce in the pan. In a small bowl, quickly stir the cornstarch into 1 tablespoon water. Add to the sauce in the pan, raise the heat to medium, and cook, stirring, until the sauce is glossy and slightly thickened, about 30 seconds. Pour the sauce over the fish, garnish with the sliced green onions, and serve.

cook's tip

A popular ingredient in southern China, black bean sauce is a thick, mildly salty sauce made from fermented black beans, usually lightly seasoned with ginger. It is sold in jars in supermarkets and Asian markets, and is commonly used in stir-fries. Black bean sauce with garlic and/or chile is also available.

seared
tuna salad

1 **Season the tuna and cook the beans**
Place the tuna on a plate and season lightly on both sides with salt and pepper; set aside. Bring a saucepan of salted water to a boil. Add the beans and cook until tender-crisp, 5–6 minutes. Drain, place under cold running water until cool, drain again, and set aside.

2 **Make the dressing**
Place a heavy frying pan over low heat to preheat. In a small bowl, whisk together the tahini, the lemon juice, 2 tablespoons water, $\frac{1}{4}$ teaspoon salt, and a pinch of pepper. Taste the dressing and adjust the seasoning with salt and pepper if necessary.

3 **Sear the tuna and finish the salad**
Raise the heat under the frying pan to medium-high and add the oil. When the oil is hot, add the tuna and cook, turning once, until browned on both sides but still rare in the center, 4–8 minutes total, depending on thickness. Transfer the tuna to a cutting board and cut on the diagonal into thin slices. Place the greens in a large bowl. Pour two-thirds of the dressing over the greens and toss to coat evenly. Arrange the greens on plates. Add a little of the remaining dressing to the beans, toss to coat evenly, then divide between the greens. Fan the tuna slices over the salads, drizzle with the remaining dressing, and serve.

Tuna steaks, about 1 $\frac{1}{2}$ lb (750 g) total weight, each about 1 inch (2.5 cm) thick

Salt and freshly ground pepper

Green beans, 6 oz (185 g), cut into bite-sized pieces

Tahini, 2 tablespoons

Lemon juice, from 1 lemon

Olive or canola oil, 1 tablespoon

Mixed salad greens, $\frac{1}{2}$ lb (250 g)

SERVES 4

17

creole
striped bass

Chile powder, ½ teaspoon

Paprika, ½ teaspoon

Dried thyme, ¼ teaspoon

Garlic powder, ⅛ teaspoon

Salt and freshly ground black pepper

White pepper

Striped bass or other firm white-fleshed fish fillets, 4, 1½ lb (750 g) total weight, pin bones removed

Olive oil, 2 tablespoons

Lemon juice, from 1 lemon

Unsalted butter, 2 tablespoons

SERVES 4

1 Season the fish
In a small bowl, combine the chile powder, paprika, thyme, garlic powder, ½ teaspoon salt, ¼ teaspoon black pepper, and ¼ teaspoon white pepper. Place the fillets on a plate and season on both sides with the spice mixture.

2 Cook the fish
In a large frying pan over medium heat, warm the oil. Add the fish and cook until well browned on the first side, about 4 minutes. Turn and cook until opaque throughout, 2–4 minutes longer, depending on thickness. Transfer the fillets to individual plates.

3 Make the sauce
Wipe any oil from the pan with a paper towel. Return the pan to medium heat, add the lemon juice and 1–2 tablespoons water, and stir, scraping up any browned bits from the pan bottom. Stir in the butter and season to taste with salt and pepper. Spoon the sauce over the fish and serve.

cook's tip

The mixture of salt, peppers, and other spices used to flavor the fish is typical of Louisiana cooking. It is a homemade version of the various packaged Creole or Cajun blends sold in stores. To save time, use 2½ teaspoons of one of these premixed seasonings in place of the chile powder, paprika, thyme, garlic powder, salt, and peppers.

cook's tip

Large fish such as salmon and
halibut can yield fillets of several
pounds apiece, which may be
sold whole, but most fishmongers
will cut them into portions of
whatever size you like. You can
substitute salmon steaks for
the fillets. Use 4 steaks, about
2 lb (1 kg) total weight.

grilled salmon with zucchini

1 **Prepare the grill**
Prepare a gas or charcoal grill for direct grilling over medium-high heat and oil the grill rack. If using a gas grill, leave one burner on high and turn the other burners off. If using a charcoal grill, bank the coals on one side of the grill.

2 **Season the salmon and zucchini**
Place the fillets on a plate and season with salt and pepper. Sprinkle with half of the thyme and drizzle with 1½ teaspoons of the oil. Place the zucchini quarters, cut side up, on a serving platter large enough to hold the fish and zucchini. Season with salt and pepper, top with the remaining thyme, and drizzle with the remaining 1½ teaspoons oil.

3 **Grill the zucchini and salmon**
Place the zucchini, cut side down, on the hottest part of the grill and cook, turning occasionally, until browned, about 3 minutes. Move the zucchini to the cooler part of the grill and continue cooking until tender, 3–5 minutes longer. Place the salmon on the hottest part of the grill until marked with grill marks on the first side, about 3 minutes. Using a spatula, turn the salmon, move to the cooler part of the grill, and cook until opaque throughout, 2–3 minutes longer. Return the zucchini to the platter and turn to coat with any remaining thyme-flavored oil. Arrange the salmon and lemon wedges on the platter and serve.

Salmon fillets, 4, 1½ lb (750 g) total weight, pin bones removed

Salt and freshly ground pepper

Fresh thyme, leaves from 6 sprigs

Olive oil, 3 teaspoons

Zucchini (courgettes) or other summer squashes, 4, quartered lengthwise

Lemon, 1, cut into wedges

SERVES 4

tilapia with sweet peppers

Olive oil, 3 tablespoons

Red, orange, or yellow bell peppers (capsicums), 3, seeded and sliced

Garlic, 1 large clove, sliced

Dried oregano, 1/4 teaspoon

Chicken or vegetable broth, 1/4 cup (2 fl oz/60 ml)

Salt and freshly ground pepper

Tilapia fillets, 4, 1 1/2 lb (750 g) total weight, pin bones removed

Paprika, 1/4 teaspoon

Flour, 1/4 cup (1 1/2 oz/45 g)

Sherry vinegar, 1/2 teaspoon

SERVES 4

1 **Sauté the peppers**
In a deep frying pan over medium heat, warm 2 tablespoons of the oil. Add the bell peppers and cook, stirring frequently, for 2 minutes. Add the garlic, oregano, broth, 1/4 teaspoon salt, and a pinch of pepper. Cover and cook until the peppers are tender and most of the liquid has evaporated, about 20 minutes.

2 **Cook the fish**
Meanwhile, place the fillets on a plate. Season on both sides with the paprika and then sprinkle with salt. Set a large, heavy frying pan over low heat to preheat. When the peppers are nearly done, raise the heat under the empty frying pan to medium-high. Add the remaining 1 tablespoon oil. Sprinkle the fillets on both sides with the flour, shaking off any excess. Add the fillets to the pan and cook until golden brown, about 3 minutes. Turn and cook until just opaque throughout, about 3 minutes. Stir the vinegar into the peppers and season to taste with salt and pepper. Transfer the fillets to plates. Spoon the peppers over and alongside the fillets and serve.

cook's tip

The pepper mixture, a simple version of a Basque *pipérade*, can be made a few days ahead and reheated. It is equally good with halibut, flounder, sole, fish in the cod family, or just about any other mild white-fleshed fish.

cook's tip

If you prefer the sauce to have a mellower garlic and herbal flavor, you can blanch the garlic and herbs. Bring a small saucepan of water to a boil, add the garlic, and cook for 1 minute. Add the parsley and tarragon and cook just until wilted. Drain into a fine-mesh sieve and set the garlic and herbs aside to cool briefly.

baked halibut with salsa verde

1 Cook the halibut

Preheat the oven to 300°F (150°C). Oil a shallow baking dish just large enough to hold the fillets in a single layer. Season the fillets lightly on both sides with salt and pepper and place, skin side down, in the prepared dish. Bake until opaque throughout, about 8 minutes; start checking the fish after about 5 minutes to avoid overcooking.

2 Prepare the sauce

In a food processor, combine the garlic, parsley, tarragon, oil, anchovy paste, and 1 tablespoon vinegar. Process until smooth, stopping once or twice to scrape down the sides of the work bowl. Season to taste with salt, pepper, and more vinegar, if desired. Transfer the fish to individual plates, top with the sauce, and serve.

Halibut or salmon fillets, 4, 1½ lb (750 g) total weight, pin bones removed

Salt and freshly ground pepper

Garlic, 2 cloves

Fresh flat-leaf (Italian) parsley leaves, 1 cup (1 oz/30 g) loosely packed

Fresh tarragon leaves, 1 tablespoon

Olive oil, 5 tablespoons (2½ fl oz/75 ml)

Anchovy paste, 1 teaspoon (optional)

White wine or sherry vinegar, 1 tablespoon, or to taste

SERVES 4

25

seared salmon
with potatoes

Russet potatoes, 1½ lb
(750 g), peeled and quartered

**Salt and freshly ground
pepper**

Milk, ¼ cup (2 fl oz/60 ml),
warmed

Unsalted butter,
2 tablespoons

Olive oil, 3 tablespoons

**Fresh flat-leaf (Italian)
parsley,** 4 large sprigs

Salmon fillets, 4, 1½ lb
(750 g) total weight, pin
bones removed

Lemons, 2, sliced

SERVES 4

1 Prepare the potatoes
Place the potatoes in a saucepan with water to cover.
Add ½ teaspoon salt, cover, and bring to a boil. Reduce the
heat to low and cook until the potatoes are tender, about
15 minutes. Drain the potatoes, reserving about ½ cup
(4 fl oz/125 ml) of the cooking water. Return the potatoes
to the pan over low heat and add the milk and butter. Using
a potato masher, mash the potatoes until creamy, adding
some of the reserved cooking water if the potatoes are too thick.
Season to taste with salt and pepper and keep warm.

2 Cook the parsley and salmon
While the potatoes are cooking, in a large frying pan over
medium-high heat, warm the oil. Add the parsley and cook
until crisp, 10–15 seconds. Using tongs, transfer to a paper towel
to drain. Add the salmon and cook until browned on the first
side, about 4 minutes. Turn and cook until opaque throughout,
2–4 minutes longer. Add the lemon slices to the pan and let
warm as the salmon finishes cooking. Arrange the potatoes,
salmon, lemon slices, and parsley sprigs on plates and serve.

cook's tip

For variety, replace the parsley
with basil, tarragon, or another
fairly sturdy fresh herb. Tiny
or especially delicate herbs such
as thyme, dill, and chervil are
more difficult to fry successfully
but are also possible substitutions.

fried catfish & greens

1 Season the catfish

Put the catfish in a shallow bowl or baking dish and season lightly with salt and black pepper. Add the buttermilk and let stand for 5–10 minutes. On a plate, stir together the cornmeal and cayenne.

2 Cook the greens

In a deep frying pan over low heat, warm 1 tablespoon of the oil. Add the onion and cook, stirring occasionally, until it begins to soften, about 10 minutes. Raise the heat to medium, add the garlic and greens, cover, and cook, stirring occasionally and adjusting the heat to prevent scorching, until the greens are tender, about 15 minutes. Season to taste with salt and black pepper and keep warm.

3 Fry the catfish

Meanwhile, in a large frying pan over medium heat, warm the remaining 2 tablespoons oil. Using tongs, lift each fillet from the buttermilk, letting any excess drip into the bowl. Roll the fillet in the cornmeal mixture, coating both sides well and shaking off any excess. Place the fillets in the pan and cook until golden brown on the first side, about 4 minutes. Turn and cook until opaque throughout, 2–3 minutes longer. Transfer to paper towels to drain briefly. Arrange the fillets on plates, spoon the greens alongside, and serve with the lemon wedges.

Catfish fillets, 4, 1½ lb (750 g) total weight

Salt and freshly ground black pepper

Buttermilk, ½ cup (4 fl oz/ 125 ml)

Fine yellow cornmeal, 1 cup (5 oz/155 g)

Cayenne pepper, ¼ teaspoon

Peanut or canola oil, 3 tablespoons

Yellow onion, 1, halved and thinly sliced

Garlic, 1 clove, sliced

Collard, mustard, or turnip greens, 2 bunches, 1 lb (500 g) total weight, trimmed and shredded

Lemons, 2, cut into wedges

SERVES 4

baked sole
with asparagus

Asparagus, 1 lb (500 g), medium-sized stalks, tough ends removed

Salt and freshly ground pepper

Sole or flounder fillets, 4 large or 8 small, 1½ lb (750 g) total weight

Unsalted butter, 1 tablespoon

Finely grated lemon zest and juice, from 1 lemon

Flour, 1 tablespoon

Chicken broth, 1 cup (8 fl oz/250 ml)

SERVES 4

1 **Bake the fish and asparagus**
Preheat the oven to 400°F (200°C) and butter a shallow 9-by-13-inch (23-by-33-cm) baking dish. Arrange the asparagus spears in a single layer in the prepared dish and season lightly with salt. Season the fillets on both sides with salt and pepper and place on top of the asparagus. Bake until the fillets are beginning to flake at the tail ends and the asparagus is tender-crisp, about 7 minutes depending on the thickness of the fillets.

2 **Make the sauce**
Meanwhile, in a saucepan over low heat, melt the butter with the lemon zest. Using a whisk, stir in the flour and cook, stirring, until the mixture just begins to color, about 3 minutes. Add the chicken broth and the lemon juice to the saucepan and whisk vigorously to break up any lumps. Cook the sauce, whisking occasionally, until thick, about 5 minutes. Season to taste with salt and pepper. Divide the fish fillets and asparagus between individual plates, spoon the sauce over the fillets, and serve.

cook's tip

Look for relatively thick, large flatfish fillets for this elegant dish. Purchase 2 of them totaling 1½ lb (750 g), and then cut them in half lengthwise to make 4 servings. Or, buy 8 small fillets totaling the same weight, and overlap pairs of fillets to make single thicker portions.

cook's tip

Let the amount and variety of fresh mushrooms be dictated by the season, availability, and your budget. Use reconstituted dried chanterelle, shiitake, or porcini in place of some of the fresh mushrooms either for variety or if the supply of fresh is limited. Substitute about 1 oz (30 g) dried mushrooms for ¼ lb (125 g) fresh.

salmon in parchment

1 Cook the mushrooms

Drain the shiitakes, remove the tough stems, and slice the caps. In a frying pan over medium-low heat, melt the butter. Add the fresh and dried mushrooms and green onions and cook, stirring occasionally, until the mushrooms are tender, about 10 minutes. If they release a lot of liquid, raise the heat to evaporate the liquid. Add the sherry and soy sauce and cook, stirring occasionally, until the mushrooms are nearly dry, 2 more minutes. Set aside to cool.

2 Make parchment packages

Preheat the oven to 400°F (200°C). Season the salmon lightly on both sides with salt and pepper. Cut 4 sheets of parchment (baking) paper, each 12 by 16 inches (30 by 40 cm), and lay them on a work surface. Bring the short sides of 1 sheet together, then fold the sheet in half and crease. Open the sheet flat and put a salmon fillet, skin side down, on one side of the crease. Spoon one-fourth of the mushroom mixture, including any buttery juices, over the fish. Bring the uncovered side of the parchment over the salmon, and starting at one end of the crease, fold the edges together to create a sealed package. Repeat to make 3 more packages, then put the 4 packages on a rimmed baking sheet.

3 Cook the salmon

Bake until the packages are puffed and browned and the salmon is opaque throughout, 6–9 minutes, depending on the thickness of the fish. Transfer to plates and serve, letting diners carefully open the hot packages at the table.

Dried shiitake mushrooms, 1 oz (30 g), soaked in water for about 30 minutes until soft

Unsalted butter, 2 tablespoons

Fresh mushrooms such as chanterelle, porcini, morel, and/or cremini, ½ lb (250 g), halved and thinly sliced

Green (spring) onions, 2, thinly sliced

Dry or medium-dry sherry, 2 tablespoons

Soy sauce, dash

Salmon fillets, 4, 1½ lb (750 g) total weight, pin bones removed

Salt and freshly ground pepper

SERVES 4

33

seared halibut with couscous

Salt and freshly ground pepper

Instant couscous, 1 cup (6 oz/185 g)

Ground cumin, ½ teaspoon

Halibut steaks, 4, 2 lb (1 kg) total weight

Finely grated lemon zest and juice, from 1 large lemon

Olive oil, 4 tablespoons (2 fl oz/60 ml)

Paprika, ¼ teaspoon

Ground ginger, ⅛ teaspoon

Green olives, ¼ cup (2 oz/ 60 g), pitted and sliced

SERVES 4

1 Make the couscous and season the fish
In a small saucepan over high heat, combine 1½ cups (12 fl oz/375 ml) water and ½ teaspoon salt and bring to a boil. Stir in the couscous and return to a boil. Cover tightly and remove from the heat. Let stand until the couscous absorbs the water, about 5 minutes. In a small bowl, combine ¼ teaspoon of the cumin, ¼ teaspoon salt, and a pinch of pepper. Season both sides of the halibut with the spice mixture.

2 Prepare the sauce
In a small saucepan over low heat, combine the lemon juice, 3 tablespoons of the oil, the paprika, the ginger, the remaining ¼ teaspoon cumin, 1¼ teaspoons salt, and a pinch of pepper. Stir to dissolve the salt. Remove the sauce from the heat and cover to keep warm.

3 Cook the fish
In a heavy frying pan over medium-high heat, warm the remaining 1 tablespoon oil. Add the halibut steaks and cook until browned on the first side, 3–4 minutes. Turn and cook until opaque around the edges, about 3 minutes longer. Fluff the couscous with a fork. Add the lemon zest and olives to the sauce. Arrange the halibut on plates, spoon the couscous alongside, drizzle with the sauce, and serve.

cook's tip

Searing is done over high heat and works best in an uncoated frying pan, such as cast iron or stainless steel. Manufacturers of

nonstick pans generally advise against cooking over high heat. If you use a nonstick pan, keep the heat level at medium-high, cook for a few minutes longer than directed in the recipe, and don't expect as much of a seared effect.

cook's tip

"Tempering" the miso with
a little of the hot stock before
adding it to the pan helps keep
it from turning granular in the
soup. Also, be sure not to let
the soup boil once the miso has
been added, or the miso will
develop a bitter taste. Look for
miso, soba, and instant dashi
at Asian markets or well-stocked
supermarkets.

miso soup with fish & soba

1 Cook the noodles
Divide the spinach among 4 deep soup bowls. Bring a large saucepan of water to a boil. Add a large pinch of salt and the noodles. Cook, stirring occasionally to prevent sticking, until the noodles are tender, about 5 minutes. Drain and divide among 4 soup bowls.

2 Make the soup base and cook the fish
Meanwhile, fill a wide saucepan with 8 cups (64 fl oz/ 2 l) water and bring to a boil. Add the dashi flakes, reduce the heat to low, and simmer for 7 minutes. Strain through a fine-mesh sieve and return to the pan. Add the soy sauce, ginger, green onions, and a pinch of sugar and bring to a simmer. Working in batches if necessary, add the fish slices in a single layer and cook just until tender but not flaking apart, about 2 minutes. Using a slotted spoon or skimmer, transfer the slices to the soup bowls.

3 Finish the soup
Bring the soup almost to a boil. Put the miso in a heatproof bowl. Ladle about ½ cup (4 fl oz/125 ml) of the hot soup over the miso and whisk to blend. Pour the miso mixture into the soup and simmer gently just until well blended; do not let boil. Ladle the soup into the bowls. Garnish with pepper flakes, if desired, and serve.

Baby spinach, ¼ lb (125 g)

Salt

Dried soba noodles, 1 package (7 oz/220 g)

Instant dashi flakes, 1 package (¾ oz/20 g)

Soy sauce, 2 tablespoons

Ginger, 4 thin slices

Green (spring) onions, 2, green tops only, sliced

Sugar

Tilapia, salmon, or halibut fillet, ¾ lb (375 g), pin bones removed and fillet thinly sliced

White miso, ¼ cup (2 oz/ 60 g)

Red pepper flakes (optional)

SERVES 4

ginger
salmon cakes

Ginger, 2 tablespoons coarsely chopped

Green (spring) onions, 2, coarsely chopped

Salmon fillet, 1 lb (500 g), skin and pin bones removed and fillet cut into pieces

Cornstarch (cornflour), 1 teaspoon

Egg white, 1

Salt

Asian fish sauce, 1 teaspoon

Canola oil, 1 tablespoon

Sesame seeds, 1 tablespoon, toasted

Soy sauce

Hot-pepper sauce

Lemon or lime, 1, cut into wedges

SERVES 4

1 **Combine the seasonings and fish**
In a food processor, process the ginger and green onions until finely chopped, stopping once or twice to scrape down the sides of the work bowl. Sprinkle the salmon pieces with the cornstarch and add to the processor with the egg white, a pinch of salt, and the fish sauce. Using quick pulses, process until the mixture resembles coarsely ground meat. Do not overprocess or the cakes will be heavy.

2 **Form and chill the cakes**
Divide the salmon mixture into 8 equal portions. With moistened hands, gently shape each portion into a patty about ½ inch (12 mm) thick. Transfer to a plate, cover with plastic wrap, and refrigerate for 5–10 minutes.

3 **Cook the cakes**
In a large frying pan over medium heat, warm the oil. Add the salmon cakes and cook until golden brown on the first side, about 3 minutes. Turn the cakes, adding more oil if needed, and cook until the cakes are slightly springy to the touch and have lost their raw color in the center, 2–3 minutes longer. Transfer to plates and sprinkle with the sesame seeds. Pass the soy sauce, hot-pepper sauce, and lemon wedges at the table.

cook's tip

Fish fillets, by definition, have no bones, but sometimes a few pin bones remain when the fillets are cut away from the body of the fish. To remove the pin bones, gently run your fingertips across the surface of the fillet—you will feel their sharp edges—then pull the bones out with needle-nose pliers or tweezers reserved for kitchen use.

oil-poached halibut with olives

1 Cook the fish

Season the fillets on both sides with salt and pepper. Remove enough of the parsley leaves to measure 2 heaping tablespoons; set the leaves aside and reserve the stems. In a saucepan or large frying pan just large enough to hold the fillets in a single layer, pour in olive oil to a depth of half the thickness of the fillets. Add the garlic, bay leaf, reserved parsley stems and a few whole sprigs to the oil. Heat the oil over medium-low heat until it reaches 170°F (77°C) on an instant-read thermometer. Carefully add the fillets, skin side down, to the pan and cook, raising the heat if necessary to keep the oil from cooling too much, until the fillets are opaque throughout, about 15 minutes for halibut and 10 minutes for salmon or cod.

2 Cook the potatoes and prepare the topping

Meanwhile, bring a saucepan of water to a boil. Add the potatoes, cover, and cook until tender, about 10 minutes. Combine the tomatoes, olives, and parsley leaves on a cutting board and chop finely. Transfer to a small bowl and stir in the vinegar to taste. Using a slotted spatula, lift the fillets from the oil, letting as much oil as possible drain back into the pan, and transfer to plates. Spoon the topping over the fillets, accompany with the potatoes, and serve.

Halibut, salmon, or cod fillets, 4, 1½ lb (750 g) total weight, pin bones removed

Salt and freshly ground pepper

Fresh flat-leaf (Italian) parsley, 1 small bunch

Olive oil, 2–3 cups (16–24 fl oz/500–750 ml)

Garlic, 1 clove

Bay leaf, 1

Red or white new potatoes, 1 lb (500 g), quartered

Oil-packed sun-dried tomatoes, 2 tablespoons well drained

Kalamata olives, 6–8, pitted

Red wine vinegar, 1 teaspoon, or to taste

SERVES 4

41

stovetop
smoked salmon

Sugar, 1 teaspoon

Salt and white pepper

Salmon fillet, 1½ lb (750 g), skin intact and pin bones removed

SERVES 4

1 Season the salmon
In a small bowl, combine the sugar, 1½ teaspoons salt, and a scant ¼ teaspoon white pepper. Place the salmon on a plate and spread the seasonings over the bone side of the fillet, applying them more heavily on the thickest parts.

2 Set up the smoking pan
Choose a cast-iron or deep frying pan (avoid nonstick) large enough to hold the fillet on a footed wire rack inside the pan, or a shallow pan where the rack rests on the rim of the pan. Cut a piece of heavy-duty aluminum foil 18 inches (45 cm) wide and 3 times as long as the width or diameter of the rack. Center the foil in the pan and press it against the surface. Sprinkle a large handful of fine hardwood smoking chips in the middle of the pan and set the rack on top. Rinse the fillet, pat dry, and place, skin side down, on the rack. Bring the edges of the foil up and crimp together to form a tent over the fillet, allowing space for the smoke to circulate and leaving a small vent open.

3 Smoke the salmon
Turn on the kitchen exhaust fan, if you have one. Heat the pan over medium-high heat until smoke begins to emerge from the tent vent. Reduce the heat to medium-low, crimp the vent closed, and cook the salmon for about 10 minutes. Open the foil to check for doneness; the salmon should be opaque throughout. If necessary, reseal and continue to cook until done. Divide the fillet into 4 portions or serve whole and carve at the table.

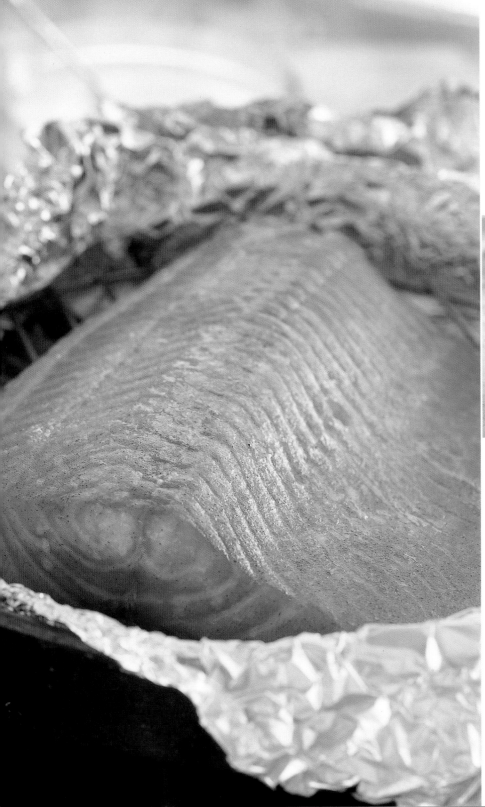

cook's tip

Use only smoking fuel intended for cooking, either hardwood chips sold for grilling or special smoking dusts packaged by manufacturers of smokers. A delicious Chinese alternative is a heaping tablespoon each raw rice, tea leaves, and sugar, a mixture that will smolder and release its own fragrant smoke.

SHELLFISH 30 minutes start to finish

warm spinach salad with scallops

Thick-cut bacon, 3 slices, chopped

White wine vinegar, 2 teaspoons

Shallot, 1, minced

Freshly ground pepper

Baby spinach, about ¾ lb (375 g)

Sea scallops, 1 lb (500 g), side muscles removed

SERVES 4

1 **Cook the bacon and prepare the spinach**
In a frying pan over medium heat, cook the bacon, stirring occasionally, until crisp, about 5 minutes. Meanwhile, in a large bowl, stir together the vinegar, shallot, and a pinch of pepper. Add the spinach and toss to coat with the vinegar mixture. Using a slotted spoon, transfer the bacon to the bowl of spinach, then drizzle 2 tablespoons of the bacon fat over the spinach and toss quickly to combine. Divide the spinach mixture between individual plates. Reserve the remaining fat in the pan.

2 **Sear the scallops**
Return the frying pan to medium-high heat and add the scallops. Cook, turning once, until golden brown on both sides but still slightly translucent in the center, about 2 minutes per side. Arrange on the spinach and serve.

cook's tip

Garlic crostini are a delicious
accompaniment to this salad
and take only minutes to prepare.
To make them, preheat your
oven to 400°F (200°C). Slice
a baguette into ½-inch (12-mm)
slices, brush with olive oil, and
place on a baking sheet. Bake
until golden, about 5 minutes.
Peel a clove of garlic and rub it
onto each warm slice of bread.

cook's tip

Look for an ale that has a sweet malt flavor and is not too bitter. The best choice for this dish is a wheat-based Bavarian-style

hefeweizen or a white ale in the Belgian tradition. A highly hopped ale, such as a West Coast style or an India pale ale, may yield a broth that is overly bitter. Also, when cooking with ale or beer, it's a good idea to use it at room temperature.

clams steamed in ale

1 Steam the clams

In a large saucepan, Dutch oven, or stockpot, combine the ale and shallot. Add the clams, discarding any that do not close to the touch. Cover, bring to a boil over high heat, and cook, shaking the pan occasionally, for 3–4 minutes. Uncover and, using a slotted spoon, transfer any fully opened clams to bowls. Re-cover the pan and continue to cook until the remaining clams open. Transfer the clams to the bowls, discarding any that have failed to open. The total cooking time will be 5–10 minutes, depending on the size of the clams.

2 Finish the broth

Add the butter to the broth and stir until melted and combined. Ladle some broth into each bowl. Serve with bread for dipping in the broth.

Wheat, white, or brown ale, 1 cup (8 fl oz/250 ml)

Shallot, 1, minced

Littleneck, Manila, or other small clams, 4 dozen, scrubbed

Unsalted butter, 2 tablespoons

Baguette or other crusty white bread

SERVES 4

shrimp with wine & herbs

Olive or canola oil,
1 tablespoon

Shrimp (prawns), 1½ lb
(750 g), peeled and deveined,
tails intact

Garlic, 2 cloves, minced

**Fresh flat-leaf (Italian)
parsley,** 1 tablespoon minced

Fresh thyme, 1 teaspoon
minced

Fresh basil, 1 teaspoon
minced

Dry white wine,
3 tablespoons

Unsalted butter,
2 tablespoons

**Salt and freshly ground
pepper**

SERVES 4

1 Cook the shrimp
In a frying pan over medium heat, warm the oil. Add the shrimp and cook, stirring, just until opaque throughout, about 4 minutes. Transfer to a plate.

2 Make the sauce
Return the pan to medium heat. Add the garlic, parsley, thyme, and basil and sauté until fragrant, about 30 seconds. Add the wine and stir, scraping up any browned bits on the bottom of the pan. When the wine has nearly evaporated, remove the pan from the heat and add the butter and a pinch of pepper. Stir until the butter melts, then return the shrimp to the pan and toss to coat with the sauce. Taste and adjust the seasoning with salt and pepper and serve.

cook's tip

For an easy pasta dish, boil 1 lb
(500 g) fresh or dried fettucine,
linguine, or spaghetti in lightly
salted water until al dente, then
drain, reserving some of the
cooking water. Toss the drained
pasta in the pan with the cooked
shrimp and sauce, adding a little
of the pasta-cooking water to
loosen the sauce.

cook's tip

If the scallops you purchase are more than 1½ inches (4 cm) thick, cut each one in half horizontally to make 2 thinner disks before you thread them onto skewers. Because the halved scallops are not as thick, they will cook more quickly and evenly.

five-spice grilled scallops

1 **Soak the skewers and prepare the grill**
Soak 4 wooden skewers in water until needed, up to 30 minutes. Prepare a gas or charcoal grill for direct grilling over medium-high heat and oil the grill rack. If using a gas grill, leave one burner on high and turn the other burners off. If using a charcoal grill, bank the coals on one side of the grill. Alternatively, preheat a broiler (grill).

2 **Season the scallops and bok choy**
Place the scallops on a plate. In a small bowl, combine the orange zest, five-spice powder, 1/2 teaspoon salt, and a pinch of pepper. Sprinkle the mixture on both sides of the scallops. Drizzle the scallops with 1 teaspoon of the oil. Place the bok choy on another plate, brush with the remaining 2 teaspoons canola oil, and season lightly with salt.

3 **Grill the bok choy and scallops**
Thread the scallops onto the skewers. Place the bok choy, cut side down, over the hottest part of the grill and cook until marked with grill marks, about 2 minutes. Turn the bok choy, move to the cooler part of the grill, and cook until tender, about 5 minutes longer. Place the skewers on the hottest part of the grill until the scallops are marked with grill marks, about 2 minutes. Turn and cook until the scallops are heated through but still slightly translucent in the center, 1–2 minutes longer. Or, arrange the bok choy on a rimmed baking sheet, place under the broiler, and cook, turning once, using the same timing. Repeat with the skewers, using the same timing. Transfer the skewers and bok choy to a platter, drizzle the bok choy with the sesame oil, and serve.

Sea scallops, 1 lb (500 g), side muscles removed

Orange zest, from 1/2 orange, finely grated

Five-spice powder, 1/4 teaspoon

Salt and freshly ground pepper

Canola or peanut oil, 3 teaspoons

Baby bok choy, 1 lb (500 g), halved lengthwise

Asian sesame oil, 1 teaspoon

SERVES 4

53

crab salad with tarragon vinaigrette

White wine vinegar,
4 teaspoons

Salt and white pepper

Fresh tarragon, 1 tablespoon
minced

Olive oil, ¼ cup (2 fl oz/
60 ml)

Mixed salad greens, ½ lb
(250 g)

Fresh lump crabmeat, ¾ lb
(375 g), picked over for shell
fragments

Mango, 1, peeled and cubed

SERVES 4

1 Make the tarragon vinaigrette
In a large bowl, whisk together the vinegar, ¼ teaspoon salt, and a pinch of pepper. Stir in the tarragon. Slowly add the oil, whisking constantly. Taste and adjust the seasoning with salt and pepper.

2 Finish the salad
Pour one-third of the vinaigrette into a measuring pitcher. Add the greens to the bowl and toss to coat with the vinaigrette. Arrange on plates. In the same bowl, combine the crabmeat, mango, and the reserved vinaigrette, and toss to moisten evenly. Mound the crabmeat mixture on the greens and serve.

cook's tip

Oven "frying," which is a good way to prepare not only shrimp, but also sea scallops and chunks of white-fleshed fish, calls for coating the food with beaten egg and crumbs as you do for deep-frying, but then cooking it in a hot oven instead of immersed in oil, yielding a similar result. *Panko*—light, flaky Japanese bread crumbs—deliver a particularly crunchy coating.

oven-fried
shrimp with aioli

1 Make the aioli
Put the garlic slices on a cutting board, sprinkle with a pinch of salt, and use the side of a large chef's knife to mash to a paste. Using the knife, scrape up the paste, transfer to a bowl, and stir in the mayonnaise and lemon zest. Set aside.

2 Season and butterfly the shrimp
Preheat the oven to 400°F (200°C). Lightly oil a baking sheet. Using a small knife, cut through each shrimp along the outside curve without slicing all the way through. Open the shrimp and press down gently to spread the two sides apart, so most of the meat lies flat and the tail curls upward.

3 Cook the shrimp
In a shallow bowl, beat the egg with the thyme and a pinch of salt. Place the *panko* in another shallow bowl. Holding each shrimp by the tail, dip in the egg, letting the excess drip back into the bowl. Then, place in the crumbs, coating both sides well and shaking off any excess. Arrange on the prepared baking sheet. Drizzle the shrimp evenly with the oil. Bake until the shrimp are opaque throughout and the crumbs are crisp, about 8 minutes. Serve with the aioli for dipping.

Garlic, 1 large clove, sliced

Salt

Mayonnaise, ¼ cup (2 fl oz/ 60 ml)

Lemon zest, from ½ lemon, finely grated

Large shrimp (prawns), 1 lb (500 g), peeled and deveined, tails intact

Egg, 1

Dried thyme, ¼ teaspoon crumbled

***Panko* or fine dried bread crumbs,** 1 cup (4 oz/125 g)

Canola oil, 1 tablespoon

SERVES 4

linguine with shrimp

Lemons, 2

Heavy (double) cream,
1 cup (8 fl oz/250 ml)

Small shrimp (prawns),
1 lb (500 g), peeled and
deveined

Fresh chives, 1 tablespoon
minced

Salt and white pepper

Linguine or fettuccine,
1 lb (500 g)

Olive oil, 1 tablespoon

SERVES 4

1 Boil the water and warm the sauce
Bring a large pot of water to a boil. Grate 1 tablespoon zest from the lemons and squeeze 3 tablespoons juice. In a small saucepan over low heat, combine the cream and lemon zest and heat until hot. Remove from the heat if the mixture begins to boil. In a small bowl, combine the shrimp, lemon juice, and chives; set aside.

2 Cook the pasta and finish the sauce
Add 2 tablespoons salt and the pasta to the boiling water. Cook, stirring occasionally to prevent sticking, until al dente, according to the package directions. When the pasta is within about 3 minutes of being al dente, warm the oil in a frying pan over medium heat. Add the shrimp to the pan and cook, stirring, until they are opaque throughout, about 2 minutes. Add the warm cream to the pan and season the sauce to taste with salt and pepper. Drain the pasta, add to the pan, toss to coat with the sauce, and serve.

cook's tip

This creamy pasta dish is quite rich, so a relatively small amount will satisfy most diners. Paired with a large, simple salad, such

as butter lettuce with champagne vinaigrette or mixed baby salad greens and cubed avocado with white wine vinaigrette, this recipe is elegant enough for a dinner party. Round out the meal with some crusty bread and a bottle of chilled Sauvignon Blanc.

cook's tip

If live lobster is easier to find,
cook the lobster by any standard
method 1 day ahead and chill
thoroughly. Another option is to
steam ¾ lb (375 g) frozen lobster
tails (typically 1 large or 2 small
tails) until the meat is opaque
throughout (8–12 minutes) and
chill them overnight.

lobster
rolls

1 Extract the lobster meat

Twist off the claws from the body. Using a lobster cracker or mallet, break the shell on each claw and remove the meat. Using a large, sharp knife, cut the lobster in half lengthwise from head to tail. Discard the black vein that runs the length of the body and the small sand sac at the base of the head. Remove the meat from the body and tail. Twist off the small legs where they join the body to check for other chunks of meat.

2 Make the lobster salad

Chop the lobster meat and place in a bowl. Add the celery, bell pepper, mayonnaise, and mustard. Stir to blend and season to taste with salt.

3 Toast the rolls

Heat a frying pan over medium heat. Butter the cut sides of the rolls. Place the rolls, buttered side down, in the pan and toast until golden brown, about 3 minutes. Transfer the rolls to plates, fill with the lobster salad, and serve.

Cooked lobster, 1, (about 1½ lb/750 g)

Celery, 1 large stalk, finely chopped

Red bell pepper (capsicum), ½, seeded and finely chopped

Mayonnaise, 3 tablespoons

Dijon mustard, ½ teaspoon

Salt

Unsalted butter, 1 tablespoon, at room temperature

Soft rolls, 4, split

SERVES 4

61

shrimp skewers with romesco

Olive oil, 5 tablespoons (2½ fl oz/75 ml), plus oil for brushing

Yellow onion, ½, chopped

Garlic, 2 cloves

Roasted red bell pepper (capsicum), ½, seeded and chopped

Paprika, ½ teaspoon

Slivered almonds, ¼ cup (1 oz/30 g)

Tomato paste, 1 teaspoon

Sherry vinegar, 1½ teaspoons

Salt and freshly ground pepper

Large shrimp (prawns), 1½ lb (750 g), peeled and deveined, tails intact

SERVES 4

1 **Soak the skewers and prepare the grill**
Soak 8 wooden skewers in water until needed, up to 30 minutes. Prepare a gas or charcoal grill for direct grilling over medium-high heat and oil the grill rack. Or, preheat a broiler (grill).

2 **Make the sauce**
In a small frying pan over low heat, warm 2 tablespoons of the oil. Add the onion and garlic and sauté until the onion is translucent, about 5 minutes. Add the roasted pepper and paprika and cook until the flavors have blended, about 5 minutes longer. Let cool slightly, then transfer to a food processor. Add the almonds and tomato paste and process until a paste forms, stopping once or twice to scrape down the sides of the work bowl. With the motor running, add the remaining 3 tablespoons oil in a thin stream. Then add the vinegar, ¼ teaspoon salt, and a little pepper and process to combine. Taste and adjust the seasoning. Transfer to a bowl.

3 **Cook the shrimp**
Thread the shrimp onto the skewers, piercing each shrimp once near the head and again near the tail to maintain the natural curve of the body. Divide the shrimp evenly between the skewers. Brush the shrimp with oil. Place on the grill rack and grill, turning once, until the shrimp are opaque throughout, about 3 minutes per side. Or, arrange on a rimmed baking sheet, place under the broiler, and cook, turning once, using the same timing. Serve on the skewers and pass the sauce at the table.

cook's tip

Most shrimp have been frozen, and they benefit from a technique called salt rinsing, which gives them a cleaner flavor and firmer texture: In a bowl, combine the shrimp with 1 heaping teaspoon salt, toss to coat evenly, and let stand for 1 minute. Rinse well with cold running water. Return the shrimp to the bowl and repeat, rinsing and draining them well before use.

thai green curry mussels

1 **Make the curry base**
Add ¼ cup (2 fl oz/60 ml) of the coconut milk and the curry paste to a wok or large saucepan and set over medium-low heat. Cut the bottom one-third of the lemongrass stalk into 1-inch (2.5-cm) pieces. Crush the pieces with the flat side of a chef's knife. Add to the wok along with the lime leaf, if using. Bring the curry mixture to a simmer over medium heat and cook, stirring occasionally, until fragrant, about 5 minutes.

2 **Cook the mussels**
Add the remaining coconut milk, ½ cup (4 fl oz/125 ml) water, and the fish sauce to the curry base and stir. Discard any open mussels that do not close to the touch, then raise the heat to high and add the mussels. When a few start to open, cover the wok and cook for 2 minutes. Uncover and, using a slotted spoon, transfer the opened mussels to bowls. Cover the wok again and continue to cook until the remaining mussels open, about 2 minutes longer. Transfer the mussels to the bowls, discarding any that have failed to open. Ladle the broth over the mussels, garnish with the basil, and serve.

Coconut milk, 1 can
(14 fl oz/430 ml)

Thai green curry paste,
1 tablespoon

Lemongrass, 1 stalk

Kaffir lime leaf, 1 (optional)

Asian fish sauce,
1 tablespoon

Mussels, 1½ lb (750 g),
scrubbed and debearded
if necessary

Fresh basil or mint leaves,
3 tablespoons slivered

SERVES 4

spicy tomato & squid pasta

Olive oil, 3 tablespoons

Yellow onion, 1 small, finely chopped

Garlic, 3 cloves, minced

Red pepper flakes, ¼ teaspoon

Fresh flat-leaf (Italian) parsley, 2 tablespoons minced

Anchovy paste, ¼ teaspoon (optional)

Crushed tomatoes with juice, 1 can (14.5 fl oz/ 450 ml)

Salt and freshly ground black pepper

Gemelli, fusilli, or other spiral-shaped pasta, 1 lb (500 g)

Squid, 1 lb (500 g) cleaned, bodies cut into strips or rings

SERVES 4

1 Make the sauce

Bring a large pot of water to a boil. In a large frying pan over medium-low heat, warm the oil. Add the onion and sauté for 2 minutes. Add the garlic, red pepper flakes, and half of the parsley, and cook, stirring frequently, until the onion starts to color but not brown, about 30 seconds. Stir in the anchovy paste, if using, and tomatoes and sauté until slightly thickened, 2–3 minutes. Season the sauce to taste with salt and pepper.

2 Cook the pasta and finish the sauce

Add 2 tablespoons salt and the pasta to the boiling water. Cook, stirring occasionally to prevent sticking, until al dente, according to the package directions. Add the squid to the pasta and cook just until opaque, 1–2 minutes. Drain the pasta and squid, add to the sauce, toss to coat, and serve.

cook's tip

A simple way to heat a serving bowl is to put it in the sink with a colander inside of it. When you drain the cooked pasta into the colander, the pasta water warms the serving bowl. This is also a good way to capture some of the cooking water, in case you need to loosen the pasta sauce.

cook's tip

Tofu is a common addition to
pad Thai. Cut ¼ lb (125 g) tofu
into small cubes and cook them
along with the shrimp. Or, for
a vegetarian version of this recipe,
omit the shrimp and Asian fish
sauce and add up to ½ lb (250 g)
tofu. Add the tofu to the wok as
directed for the shrimp.

shrimp
pad thai

1 Cook the noodles and sprouts

Bring a large saucepan of water to a boil. Add the noodles, turn off the heat, and let stand, stirring occasionally, until soft, about 10 minutes. When the noodles are nearly soft, stir in the bean sprouts. Drain the noodles and sprouts.

2 Stir-fry the shrimp and tofu

Meanwhile, in a small bowl, combine the ketchup, black bean sauce, Sriracha sauce, and fish sauce. In a wok or deep frying pan over medium heat, warm the oil. Add the minced green onions and ginger and stir-fry until fragrant, about 30 seconds. Add the shrimp and stir-fry until opaque throughout, 1–2 minutes.

3 Make the sauce

Add the ketchup mixture to the wok and bring to a boil. Pour the egg into the middle of the sauce and stir just until scrambled. Immediately add the noodles and sprouts, toss to coat evenly with the sauce, and cook until heated through, about 2 minutes. Taste and adjust the seasoning with ketchup or Sriracha. Transfer to a serving platter, arranging the shrimp on top of the noodles. Garnish with the sliced green onions and the peanuts and serve. Pass the lime wedges at the table to squeeze over the noodles.

Medium rice noodles, 10 oz (315 g)

Bean sprouts, 2 cups (8 oz/250 g)

Ketchup, ⅓ cup (3 fl oz/ 80 ml)

Black bean sauce, scant 1 tablespoon

Sriracha chile sauce, 1 teaspoon

Asian fish sauce, 3 tablespoons

Peanut or canola oil, 1 tablespoon

Green (spring) onions, 3, white parts minced and green tops thinly sliced

Ginger, 1 tablespoon minced

Shrimp (prawns), ⅓ lb (155 g) peeled, deveined, and halved lengthwise

Egg, 1, lightly beaten

Dry-roasted peanuts, 2 tablespoons chopped

Lime, 1, cut into wedges

SERVES 4

risotto with crab & lemon

Chicken broth, 2 cups
(16 fl oz/500 ml)

Green (spring) onions,
2, white and pale green parts
minced and dark green tops
reserved

Olive oil, 2 tablespoons

Arborio rice, 2 cups
(14 oz/440 g)

**Salt and freshly ground
pepper**

Fresh lump crabmeat,
½ lb (250 g), picked over
for shell fragments

**Finely grated lemon zest
and juice,** from 2 lemons

Unsalted butter,
1 tablespoon

SERVES 4

1 **Heat the broth**
In a saucepan over medium-low heat, combine the broth, dark green onion tops, and 2 cups (16 fl oz/500 ml) water. Bring to a gentle simmer and maintain over low heat.

2 **Cook the rice**
In a large frying pan over medium-low heat, warm the oil and minced green onions until the onions begin to sizzle. Add the rice and cook, stirring constantly, until all the grains are well coated, about 2 minutes. Strain all of the broth mixture over the rice. Return the saucepan to low heat, add 1 cup (8 fl oz/250 ml) water to the saucepan, and bring to a gentle simmer. Season the rice with ¼ teaspoon salt and cook, stirring every few minutes, until the liquid is nearly absorbed and the rice is tender, about 20 minutes. Adjust the heat to maintain an active simmer, not a rapid boil. Set the crabmeat out at room temperature.

3 **Finish the risotto**
When the level of the liquid in the pan drops below the surface of the rice, taste a few grains; they should be tender but still firm to the bite, and the rice should be creamy. If the rice is still underdone, add ½ cup (4 fl oz/125 ml) of the simmering water. Cook for 3–4 minutes longer, and taste again. Gently stir in the crabmeat, lemon juice and zest, and remaining ½ cup simmering water. Cook until the liquid is nearly absorbed, stir in the butter, and serve.

15 minutes
hands-on time

creamy
fish chowder

Thick-cut bacon, 2 slices, chopped

Leek, 1, halved, rinsed, and sliced

Russet potato, 1 large, peeled and cut into small cubes

Fish stock or water, 1½ cups (12 fl oz/375 ml)

Salt and freshly ground pepper

Cod or other firm white-fleshed fish fillets, ½ lb (250 g), pin bones removed and fillets cut into bite-sized pieces

Milk, 1½ cups (12 fl oz/ 375 ml)

SERVES 4

1 **Cook the vegetables**
In a Dutch oven or saucepan over medium-low heat, cook the bacon, stirring occasionally, until it renders most of its fat but is not crisp, about 4 minutes. Add the leek and potato and cook, stirring frequently, until the leek softens, 6–8 minutes. (Adjust the heat as needed so the vegetables do not brown or stick.) Add the stock, ½ teaspoon salt, and a pinch of pepper, and bring just to a boil. Reduce the heat to medium-low, cover, and simmer until the potato is tender, about 20 minutes.

2 **Finish the chowder**
Season the fish lightly with salt and pepper. Add the fish and milk to the pan and cook, uncovered, over medium-low heat until the fish easily flakes apart, about 10 minutes. Taste and adjust the seasoning with salt and pepper. Ladle into bowls and serve.

cook's tip

To clean a leek efficiently, trim
the root end, cut the leek to the
desired length, and then halve
the leek lengthwise. Hold each
half under cold running water,
carefully pulling the layers open
to wash away any dirt. Place
in a colander or on a kitchen
towel to drain briefly.

cod, leek
& potato gratin

1 Slice the potatoes, leeks, and fish
Preheat the oven to 375°F (190°C). Butter a 13-inch (33-cm) oval gratin pan or baking dish. Cut the potatoes crosswise into thin, uniform slices. Cut the leeks into slices about twice as thick as the potatoes. Season the fish lightly with salt and pepper.

2 Assemble the gratin
Arrange half of the potato slices in the prepared dish, overlapping them to cover the bottom. Season lightly with salt and pepper. Scatter half of the leeks over the potatoes, then arrange the fish over the leeks in a single layer, overlapping the slices as necessary. Top with the remaining leeks, then with the remaining potatoes. Season with salt and pepper. Pour the cream evenly over the layers.

3 Cook the gratin
Bake for 40 minutes. Remove from the oven and spoon some of the cooking liquid over the top of the gratin to moisten the potatoes and help them brown. Return to the oven and continue to cook until the top layer of potatoes is tender when pierced with the tip of a sharp knife, about 20 minutes longer. Remove from the oven and let stand for 10–15 minutes before serving.

White potatoes, 1½ lb (750 g), peeled

Leeks, 2, halved and rinsed

Cod or haddock fillets, 1 lb (500 g), thickly sliced on the diagonal

Salt and white pepper

Heavy (double) cream, 1 cup (8 fl oz/250 ml)

SERVES 4

roast bass with garlic cream

Garlic, 1 head, unpeeled

Olive oil, 3 teaspoons

Yellow onion, 1 large, thinly sliced

Striped bass, snapper, or salmon fillets, 4, about 2 lb (1 kg) total weight and at least 1 inch (2.5 cm) thick

Salt and freshly ground pepper

Heavy (double) cream, ⅓ cup (3 fl oz/80 ml)

SERVES 4

1 **Roast the garlic**
Preheat the oven to 400°F (200°C). Slice off the top of the garlic head to expose the cloves. Place the garlic, cut side up, on a square of aluminum foil, drizzle with 1 teaspoon of the oil, and wrap tightly. Set the packet upright in the oven and cook until the cloves are soft, about 40 minutes.

2 **Roast the fish**
Lightly oil a baking dish just large enough to hold the fish fillets. Scatter the onion slices evenly in the bottom. After the garlic has roasted for about 20 minutes, place the dish with the onions in the oven and roast for 15 minutes. Remove from the oven, season the fish fillets with salt and pepper, and lay the fish fillets on the onion. Drizzle with the remaining 2 teaspoons of oil and roast just until the fish is opaque, about 7–10 minutes, depending upon the thickness of the fish.

3 **Make the garlic cream**
When the garlic is tender, squeeze the pulp free of its papery sheaths into a coarse-mesh sieve. Using a spoon or pestle, force the garlic through the sieve into a small saucepan, using the ⅓ cup cream to help wash the garlic purée through the sieve. Bring the garlic cream to a simmer over low heat and reduce slightly and thicken, stirring. Season to taste with salt and pepper. Arrange the fish fillets on individual plates with the onion slices. Drizzle with the garlic cream and serve.

cook's tip

To save time, roast the garlic up to 3 days ahead of time and store it in an airtight container in the refrigerator. If you like, you can roast extra garlic to use for another purpose, such as a savory addition to mashed potatoes, a quick spread for toasted baguette slices, or to add flavor to a soup.

cook's tip

Chipotle chiles are dried, smoked jalapeños that are sold on their own or in a tomatoey vinegar-based sauce called adobo. To

adjust the heat level in this recipe, reduce or increase the number of chiles and/ or the amount of adobo sauce to taste. Store the remaining chiles and sauce in an airtight container in the refrigerator for up to 1 month.

chipotle
baked fish

1 Roast the onions
Preheat the oven to 350°F (180°C). Rub a shallow baking dish with a little olive oil. Spread the onions in an even layer in the dish and season lightly with salt. Roast, stirring once or twice, until softened and just beginning to brown, about 20 minutes.

2 Season the fish
Meanwhile, cut the chiles in half lengthwise, then finely chop the flesh. Place the chopped chiles in a small bowl, add the adobo sauce, and stir to form a paste. Place the fillets on a plate, season lightly on both sides with salt, and then rub both sides with the chile paste.

3 Cook the fish
Arrange the fillets, bone side up, on top of the onions. Bake until the fillets begin to flake apart near the tail ends, 6–9 minutes depending on thickness. Squeeze the juice from all the lime halves over the fillets and onions, garnish with the cilantro, and serve.

Yellow onions, 2, halved and sliced

Salt

Chipotle chiles in adobo, 2

Adobo sauce from chiles, 2 teaspoons

Catfish, tilapia, or other white-fleshed fish fillets, 4, 1½ lb (750 g) total weight, pin bones removed

Limes, 2, halved

Fresh cilantro (fresh coriander) leaves, 2–3 tablespoons chopped

SERVES 4

roast halibut with herb butter

Unsalted butter,
4 tablespoons (2 oz/60 g),
at room temperature

**Fresh flat-leaf (Italian)
parsley,** 2 teaspoons minced

Fresh thyme, 1 teaspoon
minced, plus 3 or 4 sprigs

Fresh chives, 1 teaspoon
minced

Lemon zest, from 1 lemon,
finely grated

Lemon juice, from 2 lemons

**Salt and freshly ground
pepper**

Yellow onion, 1 large,
thickly sliced

Halibut fillet, 2 lb
(1 kg), patted dry

Olive oil, 1½ teaspoons

SERVES 4

1 Make the herb butter

In a bowl, using a fork, beat the butter until soft and light. Add all the minced herbs, lemon zest and juice, and a pinch each of salt and pepper and beat until thoroughly blended. Taste and adjust the seasoning with salt and pepper. Set aside at room temperature. (The herb butter may be prepared up to 2 days in advance and stored, tightly covered, in the refrigerator.)

2 Season the halibut

Preheat the oven to 400°F (200°C). Oil a baking dish just large enough to accommodate the halibut. Spread the onion slices in a single layer in the prepared dish. Scatter the thyme sprigs on top. Measure the halibut at its thickest point, then rub it with the oil and season lightly with salt and pepper. Place the halibut on the onions.

3 Roast the halibut

Roast until an instant-read thermometer inserted into the thickest part of the halibut reads 120°F (49°C). Total cooking time will be about 10 minutes per inch (2.5 cm) of thickness, but start checking the halibut 5 minutes before it is scheduled to be done to avoid overcooking. Divide the fillet between individual plates, and top each serving with herb butter. Place some of the onion slices alongside and serve.

cook's tip

The herb butter is a versatile topping that complements all kinds of fish and vegetables. You can make a larger batch, roll it into a 1-inch (2.5-cm) log in waxed paper or parchment (baking) paper, wrap tightly in plastic wrap, and freeze for up to 2 months. Slice off thick disks as needed.

cook's tip

Fish curry is traditionally a simple
dish where the fish is the star.
For a heartier meal, add ½ cup
(2½ oz/75 g) frozen petite peas
when you add the fish. Or add
1 zucchini (courgette) cut into
small pieces, along with the
coconut milk. Serve the curry
over steamed rice.

indian
fish curry

1 Make the curry base

In a deep frying pan or wok over medium-low heat, warm the oil. Add the onion, garlic, and ginger and cook until the onion is soft but not browned, about 5 minutes. Stir in the curry powder and cook for 1 minute. Add the coconut milk, chiles, and 1 teaspoon salt. Cook until fragrant and slightly thickened, about 15 minutes.

2 Season the fish

Meanwhile, place the fish in a shallow bowl. Sprinkle with the turmeric and ½ teaspoon salt and toss to coat evenly.

3 Finish the curry

Add the tomatoes, lemon juice, and ½ cup (4 fl oz/125 ml) hot water to the curry base and bring to a simmer over medium heat. Taste and adjust the seasoning with salt. Add the fish to the curry and cook until the fish begins to flake apart, about 5 minutes. Transfer to plates and serve.

Canola oil or clarified butter, 1 tablespoon

Yellow onion, 1, halved and thinly sliced

Garlic, 2 cloves, minced

Ginger, 1 tablespoon minced

Curry powder, 1 tablespoon

Coconut milk, 1 can (14 fl oz/430 ml)

Jalapeño or serrano chiles, 2 small, halved and seeded

Salt

Rockfish, snapper, cod, or other white-fleshed fish fillets, 1 lb (500 lb), pin bones removed and fillets cut into bite-sized pieces

Ground turmeric, ¼ teaspoon

Plum (Roma) tomatoes, 2, seeded and chopped

Lemon juice, from 1 lemon

SERVES 4

spicy snapper with tomatoes & olives

Yellow onion, 1, sliced

Snapper, rockfish, or other firm white-fleshed fish fillets, 4, 1½ lb (750 g) total weight, pin bones removed

Salt

Limes, 2, halved

Canned crushed tomatoes with juice, 1 cup (8 fl oz/ 250 ml)

Green olives, 6, pitted and sliced

Capers, 1 teaspoon

Pickled jalapeño chiles, 1 tablespoon chopped

Fresh cilantro (fresh coriander), 1 tablespoon coarsely chopped (optional)

SERVES 4

1 Precook the onion and season the fish

Preheat the oven to 400°F (200°C). Oil a baking dish just large enough to hold the fish in a single layer. Spread the onion slices in an even layer in the prepared dish and place in the oven as it preheats to begin cooking the onion. Place the fish fillets on a plate and season lightly on both sides with salt. Squeeze the limes over the fish.

2 Cook the fish

Remove the baking dish from the oven and arrange the fillets, skin side down, on the onion. Top with the tomatoes, then scatter with the olives, capers, and chiles to taste. Cover the dish tightly with aluminum foil, return to the oven, and cook until the fillets are opaque throughout, about 10 minutes for thin fillets, 12–15 minutes for fillets about 1 inch (2.5 cm) thick. Sprinkle with the cilantro, if using, and serve.

cook's tip

Pickled jalapeños *(jalapeños en escabeche)* give this Mexican dish a piquant chile flavor. If you want a result that is less spicy, use whole

pickled jalapeño chiles and don't chop them. If you prefer fresh jalapeños, cut them in half lengthwise and put them in the dish to begin cooking along with the onion.

cook's tip

Whenever you cook with wine,
try to use a good-quality bottle
that you would want to drink,
rather than anything labeled
"cooking wine." In a recipe such
as this, where only a small
amount of wine is required, plan
to serve the same wine that
you use in the recipe with dinner.

monkfish with white beans

1 Warm the beans and cook the fish

Preheat the oven to 175°F (80°C). Trim the fennel bulb, reserving 2 tablespoons of the fronds for garnish. Use a sharp knife or mandoline to slice the bulb very thinly. Spread the beans in a deep heatproof serving dish and put in the oven to warm. In a large frying pan over low heat, warm the oil. Add the sliced fennel and cook, stirring occasionally, until it begins to brown, about 5 minutes. Season the fish lightly on both sides with salt and pepper. Add the fish to the pan with the wine, cover tightly, and cook over low heat for 10 minutes. Add the tomatoes, re-cover, and simmer until the fish is opaque throughout, about 10 minutes longer.

2 Make the sauce

Remove the beans from the oven. Using a slotted spoon, lift the fish from the pan and set on top of the beans. Spoon as much of the fennel and tomatoes as possible over and around the fish, leaving the cooking liquid in the pan. Return the pan to high heat, bring the liquid to a boil, and cook until reduced by half. Taste and adjust the seasoning with salt and pepper. Pour the sauce over the fish, garnish with the reserved fennel fronds, and serve.

Fennel bulb, 1 large

Canned white beans such as cannellini or great northern, 1 can (15 oz/ 470 g), drained and rinsed

Olive oil, 2 tablespoons

Monkfish fillet, 1½ lb (750 g), skin and membranes removed, and fillet cut into 8 pieces

Salt and freshly ground pepper

Dry white wine, 2 tablespoons

Diced plum (Roma) tomatoes, 1 can (14½ oz/ 455 g), with juice

SERVES 4

seafood
paella

Chicken broth or fish stock, 3 cups (24 fl oz/ 750 ml)

Olive oil, 2 tablespoons

Yellow onion, 1, chopped

Garlic, 2 cloves, sliced

Paella or arborio rice, 1 cup (7 oz/220 g)

Saffron threads, ½ teaspoon

Salt

Roasted red bell peppers (capsicums), 2, cut into wide strips

Mussels and/or small clams, 18, scrubbed and debearded if necessary

Shrimp (prawns), ¾ lb (375 g), peeled and deveined

Bay scallops, 5 oz (155 g)

Frozen peas, 1 cup (5 oz/155 g), thawed

SERVES 4

1 Cook the onion and rice

Preheat the oven to 400°F (200°C). In a saucepan, bring the broth to a simmer over medium heat. In an ovenproof 12-inch (30-cm) frying pan or a paella pan over medium-low heat, warm the oil. Add the onion and garlic and sauté until the onion is soft but not browned, about 5 minutes. Add the rice, crumble in the saffron, and cook, stirring, until all the grains are well coated, about 2 minutes. Pour all but ½ cup (4 fl oz/125 ml) of the broth into the pan and stir in 1½ teaspoons salt. Bring to a boil, spread the rice in an even layer, arrange the pepper strips on top, and put the pan on the lowest rack of the oven. Cook until the rice has absorbed nearly all of the liquid, about 20 minutes.

2 Cook the shellfish

Meanwhile, add the mussels to the saucepan with the remaining broth, discarding any that do not close to the touch. Cover, bring to a boil, and cook, shaking the pan occasionally, until the mussels open, about 2 minutes. Using a slotted spoon, transfer the mussels to a bowl, discarding any that have failed to open. Add the shrimp to the pan, remove from the heat, and let stand until opaque. Add the scallops and set aside.

3 Finish the paella

Press the mussels, hinge side down, into the rice. Using the slotted spoon, spread the shrimp and the scallops over the rice. Scatter the peas over all. Pour the liquid from saucepan over the rice and bake for 10 minutes longer. Let stand for 5–10 minutes before serving.

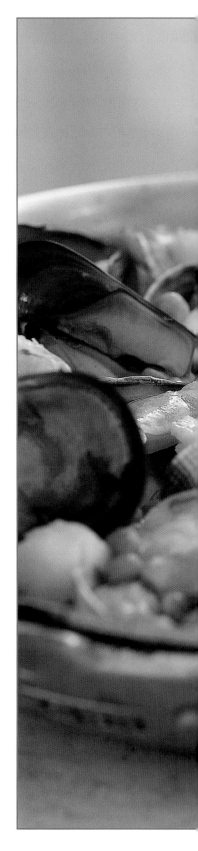

cook's tip

Serve this classic Provençal
seafood dish with its traditional
accompaniment of toasted
baguette slices topped with
rouille, a garlic-pepper sauce
related to aioli. To make a
quick version of rouille, mix
1 teaspoon minced garlic and
½ teaspoon hot paprika into
½ cup (4 fl oz/125 ml) good-
quality mayonnaise, then
season to taste with salt.

bouillabaisse

1 Prepare the soup base
In a Dutch oven or large saucepan over medium-low heat, warm 2 tablespoons of the oil. Add the onion and garlic and cook, stirring occasionally, until the onion is soft but not browned, about 5 minutes. Crumble in the saffron, add the fennel seeds and red pepper flakes, and cook for 1 minute. Add the tomatoes, stock, and 1/4 teaspoon salt. Bring to a boil, reduce the heat to low, and simmer until the onion is tender, about 30 minutes.

2 Season the seafood
Place the fish in a bowl and sprinkle with 1/2 teaspoon salt and the herbes de Provence. Add the shrimp and the remaining 1 tablespoon oil and toss to coat.

3 Cook the seafood
Taste the soup base and adjust the seasoning with salt and red pepper flakes. Add the fish and shrimp and cook over medium-low heat until the shrimp is opaque throughout and the fish begins to flake apart, about 5 minutes. Ladle into individual bowls and serve.

Olive oil, 3 tablespoons

Yellow onion, 1 large, chopped

Garlic, 4 cloves, sliced

Saffron threads, 1/2 teaspoon, crumbled

Fennel seeds, 1/4 teaspoon

Red pepper flakes, large pinch

Diced plum (Roma) tomatoes, 1 can (14 1/2 oz/ 455 g), with juice

Fish stock or vegetable broth, 4 cups (32 fl oz/1 l)

Salt

Cod, lingcod, rockfish, halibut, or other lean white-fleshed fish fillets, 3/4 lb (375 g), cut into bite-sized pieces

Herbes de Provence, 1/2 teaspoon

Shrimp (prawns), 1/2 lb (250 g), peeled and deveined

SERVES 4

the smarter cook

Adding seafood dishes to your weekly menu is a good way to put delicious, healthy meals on the table without a lot of time or effort. From spicy Creole Striped Bass to Shrimp Pad Thai, the fish and shellfish recipes in this book are simple yet inspirational, offering dishes from around the globe to brighten up even the busiest workday.

Most of the recipes in this book take less than 30 minutes from pantry to table, especially if you stick to a few simple rules, like keeping a well-stocked pantry, planning your menus for the week, and keeping an organized shopping list. Because seafood cooks so quickly, planning ahead will pay off: when it's time to make dinner, you'll be able to prepare a memorable dish in minutes, spending less time in the kitchen and having more time to enjoy home-cooked meals.

types of fish & shellfish

There are hundred of varieties of fish and shellfish. Learning the best way to cook each type will make your seafood meals more satisfying, and knowing which fish can be substituted for one another in recipes will make it easy to use what's fresh and available. Most fish are defined by texture, flavor, and fat content; shellfish are divided between two main groups, mollusks and crustaceans.

■ **Fish: Lean & Mild** The majority of fish you prepare in your kitchen will be of this variety. Some of the most common examples include bass, catfish, rockfish (red snapper), sole, tilapia, and trout. Because of the mild flavor and delicate texture of these fish, they are best when cooked with liquid or some fat to keep them moist. Suitable cooking methods include poaching, steaming, and sautéing.

■ **Fish: Rich & Full Flavored** These fish are typically those with a high oil content and a deeper color and flavor. Both salmon and tuna fall into this category, as well as sardines and mackerel. These types of fish take well to bold flavors and marinades and can withstand harsh, drier cooking methods, such as roasting, broiling, and grilling.

■ **Fish: Thick & Meaty** Size determines the members of this category, consists of fish that are too large to be cooked whole. Its members can be rich and full flavored, such as tuna, or lean and mild, like halibut and swordfish. These fish are often sliced crosswise into thick steaks, which makes them ideal candidates for grilling, broiling, and roasting.

■ **Shellfish: Mollusks** There are two main categories of mollusk: bivalves and cephalopods. Bivalves include shellfish that live within two hinged shell halves and include clams, mussels, and scallops. The pin-like shells of cephalopods are contained within their bodies. The most common shellfish in this category is squid.

■ **Shellfish: Crustaceans** These animated shellfish have legs or fins, their delicate bodies protected by a tough external skeleton. Crabs, lobsters, and shrimp (prawns) are the most popular and common shellfish in this category. Purchase live crabs or lobster for the best result in your recipe.

FISH FACTS

healthy benefits All fish are high in protein and most are low in fat. Those that are not, such as salmon, are high in healthy omega-3 fatty acids, which can lower cholesterol. For these reasons, many nutritionists advise eating fish at least twice a week.

cautions The high mercury content of some fish has caused alarm. Fish high in mercury include swordfish, shark, king mackerel, and tilefish. Doctors have warned pregnant women about eating these fish. Nursing mothers, young children, and anyone who may become pregnant may want to avoid them as well. Salmon are not included in this category, but farmed salmon can be high in toxins; if it's available, select wild salmon whenever possible.

endangered A number of the most popular types of fish are now considered endangered due to overfishing or pollution; they include Chilean sea bass, swordfish, and cod. Fortunately, today we have many choices available; ask your fishmonger for substitutes whenever possible and ensure the source is a trusted, sustainable one.

Fish and shellfish are sold in a variety of forms—fresh, frozen, or thawed—and in supermarkets, warehouse stores, or ethnic and specialty markets. In some areas, you may be able to buy the fish directly from the fishmonger or at a farmers' market. Wherever you shop, here are some tips that will help you choose the best seafood to prepare.

ask questions Fresh fish is always ideal, but some types are frozen so they can be shipped long distances. Ask if the seafood you are buying is fresh or frozen and wild or farmed.

trust your instincts Although a fish market will never smell like a bakery, it should smell like the sea, and the fish and shellfish should be chilled, preferably on a bed of ice. Avoid places with a strong, fishy smell.

check the appearances Fish fillets should glisten and shine. Dull colors and dry surfaces are warning signs that something is not right. Only purchase whole fish with clear—not cloudy—eyes and scales that are intact. Bivalves such as clams and mussels should have tightly closed shells, or shells that close when touched. Live crabs or lobsters should still be active.

be flexible Many seafood recipes have more than one option for the type of fish or shellfish that can be used. If the exact type you are looking for is not available, ask for a substitute. Or, purchase the freshest catch of the day and build your menu around it.

seafood preparation

Peeling shrimp Working with one shrimp at a time, pull off the small "legs" on the underside. Starting with the section of shell closest to the head, gently pull it up and lift it away. Leave the tail shell intact or remove it depending on your preference or as the recipe directs. To remove it, hold firmly as you pull so the meat remains.

Deveining shrimp Use a small, sharp paring knife to make a shallow cut down the center of the outer curve of the shrimp. With the tip of the knife, gently lift out the vein and pull it away, scraping if necessary.

Cleaning clams and mussels Using a stiff brush, scrub clams and mussels well under cold running water. Discard any that do not close to the touch.

Removing pin bones from fish The small pin bones found in salmon, halibut, and other types of fish fillets should be removed before cooking. Lay the fillet skin side down and run a fingertip along the center to locate the bones. Using fish tweezers or needle-nosed pliers, pull them out one by one, gripping the tip of each bone and pulling up diagonally.

Skinning a fillet Position the tail end of the fillet near the edge of the cutting board. Using a fillet knife or other long-bladed slim knife, hold the edge of the skin at the tail end securely, and position the blade at a slight upward angle between the skin and the flesh. Gently slide the blade forward along the skin, moving up the fillet, until the meat is loosened.

Cooking a fish fillet Be sure your wok or frying pan is hot before adding fish fillets. Because fillets cook quickly, a cool pan will extend the cooking time and compromise the texture of the final dish.

Testing for doneness An instant-read thermometer is useful for checking thick fish steaks or other large cuts (follow the recipe's temperature guidelines). For fillets, insert a knife or skewer into the center; it should enter easily. Shrimp should be cooked until opaque throughout; clams and mussels, until they open. Discard any that fail to open. Crab and lobster are done when their shells turn bright red.

get started

With a little advance planning and organization, preparing delicious seafood dishes can be fast and easy. The keys are keeping a well-stocked pantry (page 104), putting together a weekly meal plan, and giving careful thought to how preparing dinner fits into your schedule. With these simple strategies in place, you can work less in the kitchen and spend more time with friends and family.

- **Look at the whole week.** During the weekend, take time to think about how many meals you'll need to prepare in the week ahead. You'll want to offer variety at mealtimes, mixing up menus such as pan-seared fish fillets with green salad, spicy seafood curry with white rice, and flavorful steamed clams with crusty bread. If you shop for food on the weekend, plan to make dishes that require several fresh ingredients within a few days, saving easy meals that rely on pantry staples for later on. Getting into the habit of making a weekly meal plan will help you shop for ingredients with ease and speed and allow you to put healthy, homemade dishes on the table every night.

- **Seafood is versatile.** Healthy, delicious seafood works well in many preparations. It can stand alone, simply grilled and accompanied by a fresh green salad or roasted vegetables, or be combined with other ingredients to create flavorful stews, paellas, or pasta dishes. From an elegant lunch of fresh crab salad or a weekend barbecue of grilled salmon to an easy weeknight supper of creamy fish chowder, there is a seafood dish to suit every occasion. Try a variety of dishes and you'll find a favorite for every night of the week.

- **Let the seasons be your guide.** Most fish and seafood is caught year-round, but some varieties are seasonal. Wild salmon, including chinook (king), chum, coho, pink, and sockeye from the West Coast, are caught between late spring and late summer, for example. When planning your menu, talk to your fishmonger about availability and choose recipes that take advantage of seafood at its peak. Serve main courses with side dishes or salads that showcase seasonal produce for meals that taste fresh and flavorful.

THINK SEASONALLY

Here is a guide to using the best each season has to offer whenever you are making the recipes in this book.

spring Serve simple seafood dishes using seasonal ingredients such as leeks, asparagus, chives, and parsley. Take advantage of fresh halibut and wild salmon by preparing Roast Halibut with Herb Butter (page 82) or Pan-Seared Salmon with Potatoes (page 26).

summer Serve delicious grilled fish and seafood dishes that require minimal preparation such as Grilled Salmon with Zucchini (page 21), and vegetables, such as corn, tomatoes, bell peppers (capsicums), green beans, and squash.

autumn Serve Creamy Fish Chowder (page 74) or Warm Spinach Salad with Scallops (page 46). Prepare recipes that include hearty vegetables such as mushrooms and potatoes.

winter Serve sustaining stews, gratins, or seafood curries, like Indian Fish Curry (page 85), that call for flavorful spices. Enjoy seasonal ingredients such as sautéed winter greens as in Fried Catfish & Greens (page 29).

round it out

Once you have decided which dish to prepare as the centerpiece of your meal, choose among a wide variety of appealing side dishes to round out the menu. Keep in mind both speed and ease of preparation.

salad To save time, buy packaged, prewashed greens. Choose salad ingredients that complement the main dish: a salad with lettuce, cucumbers, and an Asian-style dressing to pair with a Thai curry, or an arugula (rocket), tomato, and shaved Parmesan salad dressed with olive oil and lemon juice to serve with grilled or fried fish.

tomatoes Slice fresh, ripe tomatoes, arrange the slices on a platter, and season them with olive oil, salt, and freshly ground pepper. If desired, sprinkle with crumbled feta cheese, olives, or chopped fresh herbs, and serve alongside grilled or seared fish fillets.

cucumbers Toss sliced cucumbers with vinaigrette and chopped fresh herbs as an accompaniment to a light seafood dish. Or, dress the slices with Asian sesame oil, rice vinegar, a pinch of sugar, and a sprinkling of toasted sesame seeds to serve alongside an Asian-inspired dish such as Ginger Salmon Cakes (page 38).

fresh vegetables You can steam, blanch, or roast many vegetables ahead of time, refrigerate them, and reheat them at dinnertime. Or, serve the vegetables at room temperature, drizzled with vinaigrette or with olive oil and lemon juice.

roasted vegetables In the time it takes to put together the main dish, you can also roast vegetables. Start with precut fresh produce, such as broccoli and cauliflower florets, butternut squash, or asparagus spears. Toss the vegetables in a little olive oil and roast in a single layer on a baking sheet at 425°F (220°C) for 10–20 minutes (depending on the vegetable), stirring occasionally. Season with salt and pepper and serve.

braised greens Buy packaged, prewashed greens, such as spinach or mixed braising greens, and cook them in olive oil. For sturdier greens such as kale, add a small amount of broth and cook, covered, until tender.

potatoes Buy small new potatoes, toss with olive oil, and sprinkle with salt before roasting as you would other vegetables (see above). Or, boil larger potatoes in salted water for 20–30 minutes and then mash them with butter, a splash of cream, and salt and pepper.

rice Cook white or brown rice ahead of time and refrigerate or freeze in resealable plastic bags.

couscous Instant couscous, available plain or in a variety of seasoned blends, takes less than 10 minutes to prepare on the stove top.

polenta Quick-cooking polenta is also ready to serve in less than 10 minutes. Make a double batch, add some Parmesan cheese, and serve half. Pour the rest into a baking pan, cover with plastic wrap, and refrigerate for another meal. When you're ready to use the polenta, cut it into squares or triangles and fry in olive oil in a nonstick pan until browned on both sides.

artisanal bread Place crusty bread briefly in the oven to warm, then slice it and serve with good-quality olive oil or room-temperature butter.

easy desserts Seasonal fresh fruit drizzled with honey, cream, or yogurt; ice cream topped with nuts and warm chocolate sauce, caramel sauce, or hot coffee; or a selection of cheeses, served with sliced apples, dried fruit, and walnuts are quick and delicious.

sample meals

IN MINUTES meals include easy recipes and accompaniments that can be put together quickly. FROM THE PANTRY meals maximize ingredients in pantry, saving you a trip to the store.

IN MINUTES	FROM THE PANTRY
Seared Salmon with Potatoes (page 26)	**Spicy Snapper with Tomatoes & Olives** (page 86)
Roasted broccoli	Roasted new potatoes
	Braised chard with garlic
Fried Catfish & Greens (page 29)	
Creamy polenta	**Shrimp Skewers with Romesco** (page 62)
Shrimp with Wine & Herbs (page 50)	Spinach sautéed with garlic, pine nuts, and raisins
Fresh fettuccine	
Butter lettuce salad	**Indian Fish Curry** (page 85)
	Petite peas
Miso Soup with Fish & Soba (page 37)	Steamed basmati rice
Mixed salad greens, cucumber, and sesame dressing	**Risotto with Crab & Lemon** (page 70)
	Butter lettuce salad with champagne vinaigrette
Clams Steamed in Ale (page 49)	
Mixed salad greens with citrus vinaigrette	**Spicy Tomato & Squid Pasta** (page 66)
Crusty bread	Spinach salad with warm bacon dressing
Fish Tacos (page 13)	**Chipotle Baked Fish** (page 81)
Black beans	Grilled corn on the cob and zucchini halves (courgettes)
Chips and guacamole	

equipment Use ceramic or glass bowls or dishes for marinating fish, as uncoated metal can give fish a metallic taste. Two large offset spatulas are useful for transferring whole fillets to and from the pan. Keep bamboo skewers on hand for grilling smaller pieces of fish or shellfish such as shrimp and scallops. If you are grilling the fish, purchase a grill basket for fillets and/or a grill screen for smaller pieces.

cooking seafood Seafood can be cooked in a number of different ways, but one rule applies to every method, from grilling to roasting to frying: Don't overcook it. Shrimp are done cooking when they turn pink. Most fish is done when it is opaque throughout and the texture is firm and flaky; the two exceptions are tuna and salmon, which are often eaten medium-rare to rare. Remove seafood from the refrigerator about 30 minutes before preparing the recipe to bring it to room temperature. Check it for doneness often to prevent overcooking, as seafood cooks quickly.

serving seafood It's best to cook fish and shellfish immediately before serving; if not served as soon as they are done, they can dry out, or, if they are held in liquid, they can overcook. Most fish and shellfish are not good candidates for reheating. Since their delicate flesh cools quickly, serve cooked fish or shellfish on platters, plates, or soup bowls that have been warmed. When serving shellfish such as clams or mussels, provide additional bowls for the empty shells.

make a template Create a reusable list template on your computer to print out when you need it. Put it on your refrigerator and fill it in during the week before you go shopping.

categorize your lists Use the following categories to keep your lists organized: pantry, fresh, and occasional. This will save you from walking down aisles aimlessly and will make it easier to delegate for quicker shopping.

■ pantry items Check your pantry and write down any items that need to be restocked to make the meals on your weekly plan.

■ fresh ingredients These are for immediate use and include produce, seafood, meats, and some cheeses. You might need to visit different stores or supermarket sections, so divide the list into subcategories, such as produce, dairy, and meats.

■ occasional items This is a revolving list for refrigerated or frozen items that are replaced as needed, such as butter, cream, milk, and eggs.

be flexible Be prepared to change your menus based on the freshest ingredients at the market. Remember: many types of fish are interchangeable.

make the most of your time

Once you've planned your meals for the week, give some thought to how you will organize your time and prepare the recipes. The more you can do in advance, the more quickly and easily a meal will come together when you are ready to begin cooking.

■ **Stock up** Over the weekend, check your pantry or refrigerator for the staples you'll need during the week. Also check your supply of basic, nonperishable ingredients, so you can improvise a quick meal or side dish. See pages 98–99 for suggestions.

■ **Shop less** If you've made a weekly meal plan, you should need to shop only two or three times a week for fresh ingredients, such as seasonal produce or seafood.

■ **Do it ahead** Do as much as you can ahead of time. For example, chop or slice vegetables or simply gather ingredients in the morning to save time in the evening. If you're entertaining during the week, check the recipe for steps that can be done ahead; making a fresh salsa, vinaigrette, or sauce in advance will save you time. Remember, too, that a pasta sauce or a soup base for a dish such as Bouillabaisse (page 93) can be made a day or two ahead and refrigerated (or frozen for a longer period), leaving you with only a little bit of work to do just before dinner.

■ **Use the grill** A gas grill or broiler (grill) can help you create flavorful dishes in minutes. Grill vegetables alongside the main dish as an accompaniment, or take advantage of the hot grill after the meal is served to grill vegetables for use the following night. Marinate seafood and vegetables ahead of time for great flavor combinations.

■ **Cook smarter** Review the recipe, taking note of any time-saving steps, such as simultaneously marinating catfish while the spicy greens cook on the stovetop (page 29), or seasoning and searing halibut while the accompanying couscous steams in the oven (page 34). Then, assemble, prep, and measure all the fresh and pantry ingredients you'll need to make the dish and get out all the equipment required. Finally, set out the serving dishes. Now, you are ready to begin cooking.

the well-stocked kitchen

Smart cooking is all about being prepared. If your pantry, refrigerator, and freezer are well stocked and organized, you'll always have a good head start on making supper. And if you keep track of what is in your kitchen, you'll shop less often and you'll spend less time at the store when you do.

On the pages that follow, you'll find a guide to all the ingredients you'll need to have on hand to make the recipes in this book, plus dozens of tips for keeping them fresh and storing them properly. Use the lists to find out what you already have in your kitchen and what you need to buy when you go shopping. The time you spend shopping and putting your kitchen in order will be time well spent—an investment in smarter cooking that pays off whenever you need to put dinner on the table.

the pantry

The pantry is typically a closet or one or more cupboards in which you store dried herbs and spices, pasta and grains, canned goods, and such fresh ingredients as garlic, onions, shallots, and any root vegetables that don't require refrigeration. Make sure that your pantry is relatively cool, dry, and dark when not in use, and away from the heat of the stove, which can hasten spoilage.

stock your pantry

- **Take inventory.** Remove everything from the pantry; clean the shelves and reline with paper, if needed; and then re-sort the items by type using the Pantry Staples list (right).

- **Start clean.** Discard items that have passed their expiration date or have a stale or otherwise questionable appearance.

- **Make a list.** Write down items that you need to replace or stock.

- **Organize the pantry.** Organize items by type so everything is easy to find. Write the purchase date on perishable items and clearly label bulk items so that you know when to discard them. Keep staples you use often toward the front of the pantry. Keep dried herbs and spices in separate containers and preferably in a separate spice or herb organizer, shelf, or drawer.

keep it organized

- **Check your staples.** Look over the recipes you selected for your weekly meal plan and check your pantry to make sure you have all the ingredients that you will need.

- **Rotate items.** Place newly purchased ingredients toward the back of the shelves, moving older items to the front where they will be seen more easily and used first.

- **Keep a list.** Regularly check the ingredients in your pantry and add depleted staples to your weekly shopping list.

QUICK FISH SEASONINGS

When you have fresh fish fillets, but you've run out of time, here are some quick and easy seasoning ideas from the pantry. Simply drizzle or sprinkle your fillets to taste with one of the following seasonings, then grill, broil, or pan-fry, and dinner is served.

INFUSED OILS
- Chile-infused oil
- Herb-infused oil
- Garlic-infused oil

SPICE MIXTURES
- Garam masala
- Curry powder
- Creole seasoning
- Chili powder (serve with lime)

VINEGARS & VINAIGRETTES
- Balsamic vinegar
- Flavored vinegars
- Purchased vinaigrette

OTHER
- Dried ground wild mushrooms, such as porcini, chanterelle, or shiitake
- Sesame seeds
- Crushed fennel seeds
- Herbes de Provence

PANTRY STORAGE

dried herbs & spices Dried herbs and spices start losing flavor after about 6 months. Buy them in small quantities, store in airtight containers labeled with purchase date, and replace often.

oils Store unopened bottles of oil at room temperature in a cool, dark place. Oils will keep for up to 1 year, but their flavor diminishes over time. Store opened bottles for 3 months at room temperature or in the refrigerator for up to 6 months.

grains & pasta Store grains in airtight containers for up to 3 months, checking occasionally for signs of rancidity or infestation. The shelf life of most dried pastas is 1 year. Although safe to eat beyond that time, they will have lost flavor and might become brittle. Once you open a package, put the pasta you don't cook into an airtight container.

fresh pantry foods Store your fresh pantry items—garlic, onions, shallots, and some roots and tubers—in a cool dark place, check them occasionally for sprouting or spoilage, and discard if necessary. Never put potatoes alongside onions; when placed next to each other, they produce gases that hasten spoilage. Store citrus fruits uncrowded and uncovered on a countertop.

canned foods Discard canned foods if the can shows any signs of expansion or buckling. Once you have opened a can, transfer the unused contents to an airtight container or resealable plastic bag and refrigerate or freeze.

PANTRY STAPLES

CANNED & JARRED FOODS

anchovy paste

Asian fish sauce

chicken and vegetable broth

chipotle chiles in adobo

diced/chopped tomatoes

Dijon mustard

hot-pepper sauce

ketchup

mayonnaise

olives

roasted red bell peppers
(capsicums)

soy sauce

tomato paste

white beans, such as cannellini

OILS

Asian sesame oil

canola oil

olive oil

VINEGARS

red wine vinegar

sherry vinegar

WINES & SPIRITS

dry sherry

dry white wine

GRAINS & PASTAS

couscous

dried pasta, such as fusilli

long-grain white rice

polenta, quick-cooking

DRIED HERBS & SPICES

bay leaves

black peppercorns

cayenne pepper

chile powder

Chinese five-spice powder

curry powder

dried oregano

dried thyme

garlic powder

ground cumin

ground ginger

paprika

red pepper flakes

salt

white pepper

FRESH PANTRY FOODS

garlic

ginger

lemons

limes

potatoes

shallots

tomatoes

yellow onions

MISCELLANEOUS

cornstarch (cornflour)

dried bread crumbs or *panko*

fine yellow cornmeal

flour

granulated sugar

the refrigerator & freezer

The refrigerator is ideal for short-term storage for your seafood and vegetables. You'll want to defrost frozen seafood slowly in the refrigerator. Dishes made with fish and shellfish are not good candidates for freezing or reheating. However, freezing is a great way to store sauces, which you can make in advance and thaw for easy seafood suppers such as Spicy Tomato & Squid Pasta (page 66).

general tips

■ Foods lose flavor under refrigeration, so proper storage and an even temperature of below 40°F (5°C) are important.

■ Freeze foods at 0°F (-18°C) or below to retain color, texture, and flavor.

■ Don't crowd foods in the refrigerator or freezer. Air should circulate freely to keep foods evenly cooled.

■ To prevent freezer burn, use only moisture-proof wrappings, such as aluminum foil, airtight plastic containers, or resealable plastic bags.

seafood storage

■ Refrigerate seafood as soon as possible after you purchase it. The best way to store recently purchased seafood is in its original wrapping in the coldest part of the refrigerator, usually near the back.

■ If refrigerating the seafood overnight, put the package into a resealable plastic bag and store it on top of ice cubes placed in a baking dish. Or, simply place the package on top of frozen ice packs.

■ Most fish should be used the same day you purchase it to keep its original flavor and texture.

■ Store live shellfish such as clams or mussels in a bowl and cover with a damp towel. Shrimp should be stored in a resealable plastic bag on a bed of ice. Never tightly wrap live shellfish or submerge them in water. As with fish, try to use shellfish within a day.

KEEP IT ORGANIZED

Once you have stocked and organized your pantry, you should apply the same basic principles to your refrigerator.

clean first Remove items a few at a time from the refrigerator and place on the counter or in the sink. Using a sponge, wash the refrigerator thoroughly with warm, soapy water, then rinse well with clear water. Wash and rinse your freezer at the same time. Replace the contents once you are finished.

rotate items Check the expiration dates on refrigerated items and discard any that have exceeded their time. Also, don't hesitate to toss out any items that look or smell questionable.

stock up Use the list on the opposite page as a starting point to decide what items you need to buy or replace.

shop Shop for the items on your list. See page 101 for tips on organizing and preparing shopping lists.

date of purchase Label items that you plan to keep for more than a few weeks, especially as frozen ones, by writing the date directly on the package or on a piece of masking tape.

fresh herb & vegetable storage

▪ To store parsley and other long-stemmed herbs, trim the stem ends, stand the bunch in a glass of water, drape a plastic bag loosely over the leaves, and refrigerate for up to 10 days. Wrap other fresh herbs in a damp paper towel, slip into a plastic bag, and store in the crisper for 3 to 5 days. Take care with fragile herbs, such as chives and basil; they bruise and discolor easily. Rinse and stem all herbs just before using.

▪ Store ripe tomatoes at room temperature for up to 3 days. If they are slightly unripe, put them in a sunny place for several days and they will ripen further. Whole fresh tomatoes should not be refrigerated; it compromises their texture.

▪ Cut about ½ inch (12 mm) off the ends of asparagus spears; stand the spears, tips up, in a glass of cold water; and refrigerate, changing the water daily. The asparagus will keep for up to 1 week.

▪ Rinse leafy greens such as spinach and kale, spin dry in a salad spinner, wrap in damp paper towels, and store in a resealable plastic bag in the crisper for up to 1 week.

▪ In general, store other vegetables, such as bell peppers (capsicums), carrots, and summer squash, in resealable bags in the crisper and rinse before using. Sturdy vegetables will keep for up to a week; more delicate ones will last for only a few days. Remember to store root vegetables such as potatoes at room temperature in a cool, dark place.

wine storage

▪ It is always best to cook with wine that you would actually drink, or "table wine." Avoid purchasing anything labeled "cooking wine," as it is generally poor quality and can affect the flavor of your dish.

▪ Once a wine bottle is uncorked, the wine inside is exposed to air, eventually causing it to oxidize and taste like vinegar. Store opened wine in the refrigerator for up to 3 days. Use a vacuum wine pump to stopper the bottle if you have one.

index

Oxmoor
House®

OXMOOR HOUSE

Oxmoor House books are distributed by Sunset Books
80 Willow Road, Menlo Park, CA 94025
Telephone: 650 321 3600 Fax: 650 324 1532

Vice President/General Manager Rich Smeby
National Accounts Manager/Special Sales Brad Moses
Oxmoor House and Sunset Books are divisions of
Southern Progress Corporation

WILLIAMS-SONOMA

Founder & Vice-Chairman Chuck Williams

THE WILLIAMS-SONOMA FOOD MADE FAST SERIES

Conceived and produced by Weldon Owen Inc.
814 Montgomery Street, San Francisco, CA 94133
Telephone: 415 291 0100 Fax: 415 291 8841

In collaboration with Williams-Sonoma, Inc.
3250 Van Ness Avenue, San Francisco, CA 94109

Photographer Bill Bettencourt
Food Stylist Kevin Crafts
Photographer's Assistant Angelica Cao
Food Stylist's Assistant Alexa Hyman
Text Writer Kate Chynoweth

Library of Congress Cataloging-in-Publication data is available.
ISBN-13: 978-0-8487-3144-1
ISBN-10: 0-8487-3144-1

WELDON OWEN INC.

Chief Executive Officer John Owen
President and Chief Operating Officer Terry Newell
Chief Financial Officer Christine E. Munson
Vice President International Sales Stuart Laurence
Vice President and Creative Director Gaye Allen
Vice President and Publisher Hannah Rahill
Art Director Kyrie Forbes Panton
Senior Editor Kim Goodfriend
Editor Emily Miller
Designer Andrea Stephany
Associate Editor Lauren Hancock
Assistant Editor Juli Vendzules
Production Director Chris Hemesath
Color Manager Teri Bell
Production and Reprint Coordinator Todd Rechner

A WELDON OWEN PRODUCTION
Copyright © 2007 by Weldon Owen Inc. and Williams-Sonoma, Inc.
All rights reserved, including the right of reproduction in
whole or in part in any form.

Set in Formata
First printed in 2006
10 9 8 7 6 5 4 3 2 1
Color separations by Bright Arts Singapore
Printed by Tien Wah Press

Printed in Singapore

ACKNOWLEDGMENTS
Weldon Owen wishes to thank the following people for their generous support in producing this book:
Heather Belt, Ken DellaPenta, Judith Dunham, Marianne Mitten, Sharon Silva, and Kate Washington.

Photographs by Tucker + Hossler: pages 30 and 78

Cover photograph by Tucker + Hossler: Bouillabaisse, page 93

A NOTE ON WEIGHTS AND MEASURES
All recipes include customary U.S. and metric measurements. Metric conversions are based on
a standard developed for these books and have been rounded off. Actual weights may vary.